Following in His Footsteps

How to hear God's voice and follow Jesus' calling in our lives

Naomi Smyth

malcolm down

PUBLISHING

Cover design by Esther Kotecha
Front-cover painting by George Jones
Art direction by Sarah Grace

Printed in the UK

In loving memory of our friend Ashley Houston
who went to be with Jesus on 28th April 2022.

Contents

Chapter One
From Heavenly Place to Humble Abode

*But the Spirit produces love, joy, peace, patience, kindness, goodness, faithfulness, **humility** and self-control.*
Galatians 5:22-23 (GNT)

September 2016

I can still see that temporary room after all these years; it was heavenly. Crisp white sheets and black silk flowers in the corner of each pillow, various shaped cushions all sitting under voiles draped at the head of the majestic looking bed. This resting place was extremely comfortable. It was hard to believe that I was the 'Hidden Homeless' as my suitcase lay open on the floor, making it easier to grab my clothes. Another smaller case sat propped against the radiator in that little bedroom holding all the shoes I owned. A chest of drawers acted as a place to set out all my make-up, and a bedside table housed my jewellery.

My very good friend had helped me in my hour of need. I had walked away from the man I loved because he had a drink issue. It had greatly affected our relationship. God's words to me at this time were, 'Let him go, as I will never let him go.' So I obeyed, as I knew that slowly but surely it was destroying me to stay. I had travelled from Newtownards to Donaghadee in Northern Ireland in order to reach my friend's flat. She was a great help to me and a true friend in my time of trouble.

So there I was at this conjuncture in my life. When people say the word 'homeless', images often flash across people's minds of an unwashed man lying on a street corner with a bottle of wine in a brown paper bag. In my lifetime I had pioneered teams onto the streets of Belfast with a heart to 'befriend' the men and women we would find on a Friday night, sleeping rough and surviving in whatever life had thrown at them. I had witnessed homelessness from both sides of the fence, making friendships with those who had found themselves destitute. Also in my own lifetime I had been in two women's hostels and rebuilt my life after two difficult marriages.

The homelessness I was experiencing this time was a different kind. It involved having a comfortable place to stay, but a lack of comfort of not knowing what the future held and experiencing my whole world turned upside down.

The first few days were very tearful as I let go of the man I loved. I had felt pushed to extremes; experiences such as sleep deprivation and dealing with a contention only drink conjures up and the pain of watching the man I loved destroy himself with vodka. The reality was he carried his own set of reasons for drinking and I came to understand that only he could work that out with the help of a good counsellor and trust in God. Without drink he was this warm and caring man. In the evenings when I sat with him I would nestle into his arms and his heat emanated a security I had craved for all my life.

After everything I had encountered in my life, I gravitated towards him, thankful for that warmth. God had healed away past pain but with this man his sense of humour always kept me alive, disallowing me to slip into depressions I had once known before God's healing touch.

On a practical level, I knew from previous experience of being in a difficult relationship and having been in two women's hostels that I needed to make a housing application. At first I thought that I was to apply to Belfast Housing, but then God gave me a picture of a red traffic light. So I visited Bangor Housing Executive and filled in the necessary forms. At this point of the journey I could see that God was keeping me in County Down (no doubt because at some stage the man in my life would turn from his wrong path). I'm originally from Belfast and naturally gravitated towards there whilst looking for a place to live, but I was to be obedient in God's greater plan.

The first five days I took off work as annual leave as I worked in the Health Service. It wasn't long before I was faced with the reality that I needed to take more time off with stress. I sought advice regarding a holiday. Originally, my boyfriend and I were meant to go on a holiday together but instead this was changed so that his daughter could go with him. In the midst of my turmoil I had visited a women's aid hostel. (This wasn't because I had been harmed physically. I just knew they were very good in the area of self-help, therefore I availed myself of their counselling.) In a picture on the wall of where I was counselled I noticed one seat and a table in a Spanish location. I knew that somehow, someway, I was to holiday alone. Even though we weren't going together to Bellevue, a resort in Alcudia, Majorca, I still felt very drawn to it. When I looked at the photos of the resort online I felt as if I would feel safe there on my own, so I booked it.

Meanwhile, back at my temporary accommodation, my friend helped me to look forward to a new life. She was a wonderful help to me at this time. She understood because she had travelled a painful road herself and knew God had helped her on her own journey.

God also communicated that my boyfriend and I were like two little love birds. In my boyfriend's apartment there was a birdhouse that held our key rings: his red bird would fit into one space and then my green bird would fit into the other space. There was a magnet that held them there. Before my boyfriend and I had split up his red bird had fallen off his key ring and was lost. We both understood the significance of this, as if everything was falling apart. In desperation

I had ordered another birdhouse and two keyrings. When they arrived, it was a white bird and a pink bird. It wasn't long before God was communicating the significance to me. My boyfriend at that time was the white bird; he was about to undergo a cleansing. I was the pink bird about to heighten my understanding of all the attributes of who I was, my femininity and all areas of self-awareness in order to live a more balanced life.

I met with one of my boyfriend's daughters, and let her know I was planning on going on holiday to the same place that her dad was going. The dates overlapped by one day. I was going to arrive the day before my boyfriend and his daughter were leaving. It was suggested that we meet up. I thought about it and arranged with his daughter to meet for a meal. My boyfriend knew nothing about it. On the way to the airport my boyfriend phoned me crying saying it could all be worked out. I loved him a lot but felt that God had given me strong guidance to holiday alone.

When I arrived in Majorca my boyfriend had been there for twelve or thirteen days. I found out what room they were in and made my way to the door. His daughter knew I was coming so let her dad open the door. I nearly gave the man a heart attack as he staggered back in amazement at my presence there. We hugged and not long after we all sat down to a meal outside. This was a beautiful evening and one I will never forget. I waved them off. Thankfully they got a coach (although they almost missed it) to take them to the airport.

Opposite the front door of my spacious apartment was a mountain. God knows I love mountains. I took in their beauty, to me speaking of his magnitude. In the distance as you looked out from the veranda you could see a mountain range: three large mountains, three medium and an array of smaller ones. Close to the veranda lay a good-sized swimming pool with a carpet of lush green grass leading up to it. Dark-green trees dotted the mid-blue sky; the odd white fluffy cloud broke up the hues of green and blue that lay before me. This was truly another heavenly place.

The apartment was basic but comfortable. There were four seats on the veranda and a round table. In the dining area another table with four chairs, which sat close to a swinging door that took you into a kitchen. In the main living room an archway led into two bedrooms and a bathroom. I felt truly blessed.

I unpacked and settled myself in. Later that day I did a shop in the local Spar. I spent over twenty euros so I was given a box of pastries. After leaving my food at the apartment I walked into Alcudia. The first thing I spotted was a red mini with a black roof. I was amazed at this as I had secured the exact same thing back home and would pick it up on my return. I had always admired them but never thought for one moment that I would drive one. I felt as though it was a sweetener in amongst the difficult days that would lie ahead.

Every day in Spain was different. One day I would go to the old city of Alcudia with a packed lunch and enjoy the old Spanish streets and shops. Another day I would ride the 'Ting Ting', a little train that chugged about to let you see the surrounding area. Another day I would venture to the beach and read under a tree in the shade. At the same time every day I would go back to the apartment for a siesta and sleep from noon to 3pm or 4pm. I ate out occasionally, but often made my own food and ate it out on the veranda. I had brought my thermos mug and it kept my tea warm. Anyone who knows me knows I drink my tea very slowly and very often just half a cup. This kept my tea warm enough to drink it all.

Some of the time I journaled and enjoyed receiving revelation from God. It truly felt like I had set myself apart. One evening as I sat looking out from the veranda, I was surprised by the mountain range in the distance. The sun was shining on the mountains and it lit them up. As I looked God quickened something to my spirit. 'When you go home you will have mountains to face, but I will be with you.' I grabbed a pen and started to sketch out the mountain range. As I studied it I realised that the first mountain was a large mountain; when I returned home I knew I would need to position myself to start back to work in Belfast. At that time I lived in Donaghadee and it was too far away for my work. I was able to write various revelations beside each mountain. This map helped me in the following months.

We have a God who cares about every detail of our lives. There are times in life we do not need a map, the path is obvious. For me, God knew I needed this for the difficult months ahead as I trusted him for my future.

In the mountain guidance there was also another message. Moses had once trekked up a mountain to bring God's direction to his people. Moses had encountered a stiff-necked people determined to do things their own way. When God showed me this I knew my journey with my boyfriend wasn't going to be plain sailing. In the following months I would truly have to let him go as he insisted on 'drinking in moderation'. Before we parted for eight months I gave him his white bird keyring. Only God could do the cleansing now. He eventually would lay down the vodka and seek the help he needed. Meanwhile, I set my eyes on godly pursuits.

On holiday I also had time to think about this book and for the first time the chapters took form. I already knew that the book was about a vision I received twenty years ago, but I didn't know how I was to form the embodiment of what was shown to me.

When I arrived back in Northern Ireland I jumped into my car which I had parked at the airport. I got to my friend's heavenly place and enjoyed an amazing sleep in that wonderful bed!

The next day I collected my mini and, true enough, it did alleviate the difficulties I was to face in the following weeks and months. My friend had offered for me to stay at his house. This was to be my next temporary home. My friend had a few animals and strangely enough it reminded me of the manger. (My friend has a good sense of humour so I know I'm not insulting him.)

I called this chapter 'From Heavenly Place to Humble Abode' because in the case of Jesus he chose to come from his heavenly place down to earth for the sake of saving the world.

In Genesis it tells us that mankind was made in 'OUR' image, meaning the Trinity. That is the Father, the Son and the Holy Spirit. The Trinity created the world, and then Jesus was requested by the Father to come to earth, to bridge the gap between the Father and humanity once the communion had been broken by Adam and Eve in the Garden of Eden.

When we receive Jesus as the divine answer from heaven to a broken relationship with God, we understand that we are incapable of working our way into heaven through good works or church attendance. Simply, we put our trust in the 'One True High Priest' who has taken the sins of the world. He becomes our mediator and we can once again fellowship with a loving Father.

Additionally, if we understand that he was FIRST with the Father in heaven then we will understand that he gave up so much to come from that heavenly place down to a humble place, not just a manger but as small as a tiny seed in the womb of Mary. What vulnerability.

Every time we ourselves travel a path from greatness to a lowly path, we can take heart that we are following in Christ's footsteps. Never despise the days of small things. All paths have lessons.

God's ways are not our ways and he works all things together for those who love him. I embraced my humble abode knowing it was one of my mountains. Soon I was to return to work in Belfast . . . and traverse more mountain paths.

Chapter Two
Destiny

But the Spirit produces love, joy, peace, patience, kindness, goodness,
***faithfulness**, humility and self-control.*
Galatians 5:22-23 (GNT)

2001

I had been married for five years to my first husband. The marriage had been an abusive one that went on to reach the ten-year mark only because I didn't believe in divorce. In the very end God showed me clearly his own divorce with Israel. As a nation she chose not to change and God showed me that when free will is used correctly, it is a wonderful thing to behold, but when used incorrectly it can damage another's life. Israel broke covenant with God. My husband did the same, he did not love . . . rather he controlled and abused. I forgive him but at a certain stage in my life God gave me a powerful vision of a jack-in-the-box. A hand would come and push the button and the jack-in-the-box would jump out with a painted-on smile and move back and forward on a spring. When my first husband man-handled me for the last time God showed me this vision again . . . he took the jack out of the box, took off the spring and put on a pair of legs. He then motioned for the figure to walk away. When I received this I knew that God was giving me permission to walk. At the time, I had started playing guitar and I wrote a song called 'A Great Pair of Legs'. It was all about having the freedom to walk away.

God had taken me through various healings as I managed a roller coaster of emotions in my first marriage. God works in mysterious ways; every abusive encounter only helped me to unlock various emotions that lay trapped in my hidden childhood. As I faced the emotions of that day I very often faced the turmoil that lurked in my childhood years. Bit by bit God broke me free, allowing me to face the dark realities that lay within.

Some of the healings were about apparent simple things, some of which I thought, 'Does that really matter?' But very often the Holy Spirit would encourage me, that even what I saw as small and insignificant had the ability to cripple me emotionally and for this reason he wanted it pulled out by the root. Basically, any lies we believe about ourselves only serve to assist Satan, as he is the father of lies. God is Truth and he wants his children to know who they truly are.

One day, sitting on a couch in our kitchen in Carrickfergus in Northern Ireland, I struggled with the light shining in through the window. I knew the irrational feelings I had were not normal. Months previously I had been involved in a ministry which helped deal with unresolved issues in your life. I knew I was experiencing a 'trigger', so I asked the Holy Spirit to reveal the root of my uneasiness.

When I closed my eyes I found myself revisiting my experience of the womb, or more accurately a position in the birth canal. The overwhelming feeling was fear. I didn't want to venture down the birth canal (thus the lack of appreciation for the light). In my case I was a breach birth. I almost died as the umbilical cord wrapped itself around my neck. They had pushed me back up only for me to be born a week later on New Year's Day.

Basically, in the birth canal I didn't want to travel back down. This had played out in my life. Any new adventure instead of being exciting was filled with anxiety for me. So how did God fix this? He didn't re-write history but rather he showed me what happened from a different perspective. The bad news was I had nearly lost my life and I will go into more detail about this in a moment, but the good news is that God showed me two angels standing at the end of the birth canal waiting for me to enter the world. He reminded me of the scripture, 'For He will give His angels [especial] charge over you to accompany and defend and preserve you in all your ways' (Psalm 91:11 AMPC). If you truly believe that God gives angels charge over you . . . it seriously changes your life! You no longer feel a fear or dread facing anything new. Something lifted off me that day. I also prayed against a spirit of death as I believe these things can attach themselves to us, even giving us a dark countenance. His healing touch changed my life. Not only did I look different in future photos but I felt lighter.

I have been to Uganda three times. Interestingly, they call their birthday 'womb escape'. I think this is a wonderful name for the day we were born. We escape from the familiarity and warmth of a womb into a cold, unknown world, born to make a difference.

I mentioned almost dying. This is what was revealed to me. There was something in common for both Jesus and Moses. Satan had sought their lives. Moses was going to deliver the Israelite people and Jesus was going to deliver a whole world. Satan moved in a certain form . . . through earthly powers to seek the life of the firstborns because he knew if he killed them at birth, then the deliverances would not take place. God, of course, had his hand on his servant Moses and his Son Jesus.

When you are a son or daughter of the Most High God, don't underestimate the lengths that Satan will go to keep you from your destiny. If you have a heart after God then you will choose ministries that bless his heart. Satan knew the ministries I would choose and he knew that lives would be changed. Of this I have no doubt. Does this make me special? No, it doesn't, even though I am special in the sight of my heavenly Father, but rather the revelation I received helps me to understand that as Christians we ARE in a battle.

Each of us is powerfully and wonderfully made by a loving Father who never makes mistakes. That means he had something in mind when he formed you in your mother's womb. Maybe you have never sat down with the creator of this universe and asked him the question 'Why am I here?'

Sometimes we can work day in, day out, but that's not who we are. For me, most of who I have been and who I will be is not my day job. It has been outside of my work. It has been in a ministry for the homeless, or a ministry to reach out to those in the church others don't bother with, or an activity camp, or a mission trip.

In order to find your DESTINY you will need to find Direction. Seek God's face. Enquire of him. He knows you better than anyone and what makes you tick. It will become clear to you. What are you passionate about? What struggles have you encountered? What messes have you found yourself in? Your mess can become your message.

Enjoy a balanced life. Never do one thing excessively. Divide your time. Give God the first of your day. Write down the different areas of your life and balance them out. If you feel like you are losing yourself, take some time out and name things on a page or in a book that are YOU.

Seek first the kingdom. It's true: seek after Jesus and other things will add to your life. In Psalm 1 we are told about a tree planted by the water's edge. Indeed, Jesus is the sap that nourishes our very soul. In John 15:4 it says, 'Abide in me' (KJV). There is a reason for this: if we don't abide in Jesus then we slip back into our old nature, desiring the things of this world once again. In a kingdom walk we will always be challenged to embrace the new as the Father cuts off even the good branches, as we may in our worldly wisdom think that hanging onto something familiar is the way ahead, but God knows best.

It is not my intention to make the heavenly Father out to be like someone out of *The Texas Chainsaw Massacre*! Rather better to point to a tree or shrub that has been wisely pruned; years later that same tree or shrub looks amazing! It also gets admiring glances from every passer-by. When we shine for Jesus that light will always emanate back to the Source for the glory to go back to him.

Time out. Time spent with Jesus is time well spent. We spend so much time sleeping, working, watching TV and even eating. If we were to divide up our day into how little we give to God it can make us blush as Christians. When we spend time with God, he will always impart something of himself to us.

Identity. Do you know who you are? If you struggle with this ask God to reveal and heal. Jesus said, 'If you want to know the Father, look at me.' This helped me a lot in my early years as a Christian. I read through the gospels getting to know Jesus. Every time Jesus healed or helped someone I knew that the Father had exactly the same love, compassion and heart as his Son. It is our job as Christians to seek out the nature of the Trinity. Put it this way: if you were going for a job it is likely the first interview question would be about the company or organisation and what you know of them. How much more do we need to know about the ones we claim to be adjoined to and part of their kingdom?

Know who you are by knowing who they are (the Trinity). You will start to see the correlation. As you hunger for Christ, his nature becomes your nature. It's true, those you rub shoulders with . . . they will rub off onto you.

New Adventures. As you do all of the above new adventures will start to unfold. As you listen to the whispers of the Holy Spirit he will guide you and lead you into new adventures. With every new adventure there is always trust. God can give you a clear idea of what to do or where to go, or he can give a skeleton image, only the muscles, sinews, flesh and skin making their way on to the embodiment of the dream as you walk by faith. Be still and know HIS voice, know his heart and know his dreams.

You and others. As you sort out yourself you can then love others out of a pure heart. In God's word it says 'love your neighbor as you love yourself'. If you haven't learnt to love yourself you will find it hard to love others. You will find yourself judging quickly and looking at others with less than a godly heart. Learn the way of forgiveness. Learn to say in your heart, 'They knew not what they were doing.' In this you will follow Christ.

So what is your destiny? Enjoy finding this out from the One who knows you better than anyone. Enjoy the walking and the talking, remembering he also wants to dine with you and to live in every area of your life. To be your guide, your comforter, your brother . . . He is waiting for you to come to him and learn from him and walk in his footsteps.

Chapter Three
The Hidden Years

*But Spirit produces love, joy, peace, **patience**, kindness, goodness,*
faithfulness, humility and self-control.
Galatians 5:22-23 (GNT)

September 2016

Between the ages of twelve and thirty we have very little account of the years of Jesus. I call these 'the hidden years'. If we think that nothing happened in those years, then we are naïve. God always works in the background and wastes nothing. Often when we think that nothing is happening, that is the very time God is working his miracles. In these times we can feel redundant, sometimes wondering what God is playing at, but in those barren years we tend to find out exactly what we believe and often a hunger grows for more of God and his kingdom.

In my hidden years I found out that I gathered a lot of my confidence from having a job. Once I wasn't working I found my insecurities rise to the surface. Whatever God was doing in those years it was as if I had fallen off the planet. I'm sure friends and family thought I had been abducted. Yet it was in those years that God gave me some very profound healings and revealed to me who he was.

Never be afraid of setting yourself apart with the Almighty. It reminds me of being in love. When you are in love you want to spend every waking hour with that person. You want to eat with them, walk with them, and talk with them. Sometimes people are worried about you because that person becomes the only one you want to be around.

When we first become Christians it can be like this. Suddenly we have a desire to walk, talk and even eat with Jesus. We want to know everything about him, what pleases him, what blesses his heart.

There is also a euphoria that can fill our hearts when we love him with everything we have. It overflows into worship and even the raising of our hands. I have heard people who don't understand and criticise Christians for outward shows of affection for their Lord, but it is normal! When we love someone that much . . . we show it. Football fans think nothing of shouting out, singing and repeating words of worship for their team. It's no different with Team Jesus; we also shout out and sing out . . . because we will never walk alone.

So it is in the hidden years that you find out if you truly believe what is written in his word. Very often when we are hidden we are not even 'doing' very much, which definitely hits into any religious spirit that may have attached itself to us in the early years of our walk with God. This can come purely through being at church! We can wrongly learn that if we are 'doing' we are succeeding. When you come out of the 'doing' and feel empty, this is a sure sign that you have put your trust in something other than Jesus. When I first had this revelation, it set me free that God loved me whether I did nothing or if I carried out beautiful acts for the advancement of his kingdom. If you think the latter is purely what pleases God then you fall into a self-righteous state and a mentality of 'works' that is unhealthy for the Spirit-filled Christian.

In a nutshell, the hidden years deals with our ego! Our identity is also meant to be in Christ. We are meant to be hidden in him. Sometimes we can be chomping at the bit to let others know what giftings we have. Don't get me wrong, there are occasions where we are not going to grow or be used of God in some places and God will guide you to pastures new, but sometimes God is all about the timing! Remember what Mary said to Jesus about the lack of wine at the wedding (John 2:1-11). She knew her son could fix the problem . . . but he was reluctant to show what was on the inside too early. I often wonder why. I believe it was timing and also I believe that Jesus only did as his Father told him. In this case it was his mother, but he did as she asked so it must have got the OK from the Father or Jesus wouldn't have done it.

Another type of hidden is sickness. Do you know that part of Psalm 23 that says, 'He makes me to lie down in green pastures'? Well that has happened to me on occasions and I have noticed a pattern. Sometimes my life becomes crazy busy and the Shepherd has to put this particular sheep on her back. Oh, don't get me wrong. I am not suggesting that God gives sickness. I am saying that when we burn the candle at both ends and we don't set in enough 'set apart' time with God, we can become dry and burnt out. We also lose the ability to hear what he is saying. I call it the Christian MOT and we all know what happens to our cars if we don't take them to get serviced and oiled: they don't make it. Very often, by doing something simple we can avoid the breakdown.

Also, on a few occasions when my car needed an MOT, I didn't always have the money to service it. The mechanic at the centre would point out what had failed my car. My re-sit was only £18.50, cheaper than paying for a mechanic to tell me of things that I didn't need to fix. Do you know that God is our creator . . . he knows our every point of breakdown. If we go to him first then he can let us know straight away what is lacking and what will fail us. He will not take advantage or make a bigger issue of something that can be easily fixed.

That's why I don't fuss when I'm sick now. It's usually something I need to attend to. It's not the ideal, but I know that I need to take a good look at things.

Another scriptural context for the hidden years is Joseph's story. Joseph revelled at the dream given to him by God, relaying how his brothers would one day bow at his feet. The out-workings of this word contained a great deal of pain and yes – you've guessed it – hidden years. It would be a long time before Joseph would be recognised in the light of his original dream. The purpose behind his brothers bowing down to him would later fit into the proper context of a starving nation and God's greater plan of redemption for a people who feared for their livelihoods.

Therefore, when God gives us a vision or a dream it is more than likely to help a certain group of people and it may take years to come into fruition. So when we experience the pit, false accusation, or being over-looked, we must hang on to the original vision or the dream given to us. In the hidden years he is building our characters and making us fit for the purpose of what he has called us to.

In these things, we surrender to his Master plan. So what we don't know about Jesus in his hidden years we can guess, although some would argue with this approach. We can read between the lines and know that Jesus was hunted down in his toddler years (aged two to be exact), lived a humble existence learning the craft of carpentry, suffered the loss of his earthly father, understood how it felt to be a prophet in his own town but not always listened to, living with a knowledge beyond his years, a life of singleness, misunderstanding, rejection. So it is in the hidden years that Jesus was prepared for his Grand Finale. Yes, he was heralded with the words 'Hosanna' and then, in a short space of time, his crucifixion was demanded. Jesus humbly came to this earth as a seed in Mary and then humbly gave up his life.

'Heavenly Father, may we understand the full significance of our "Hidden Years" as they shape and mould us for your greater purposes. Amen.'

Chapter Four
Wilderness Walk

*But the Spirit produces love, joy, **peace**, patience, kindness, goodness,*
faithfulness, humility and self-control.

Galatians 5:22-23 (GNT)

1996

The autumn leaves crushed underneath my feet as I walked beside a little river in a place called Glynn, just outside Larne in Northern Ireland. The little cottage that my first husband and I lived in sat only a hundred yards away in the main village of Glynn, County Antrim in Northern Ireland.

It was a lovely little place with lots of character and a long garden out the back that held the treat of blackberries to make jam when the hours felt long, and a flat griddle in the corner cupboard of the kitchen to make potato bread, keeping the cost of our food shopping down as we lived on one wage.

We had just left a church under difficult circumstances. God had led us out and given very clear instruction. It had been a very painful experience as the relationships we once had with people in the church now lay fragmented. We had lived in the church as caretakers. As soon as we had given a month's notice the guidance from God was strong to give away all our large items. Different friends needed various items. Soon our suite was gone, table and chairs, bed, washing machine, everything, even some of our smaller items. I gave a drill away to a shepherd who used to come and tend his flock in the field opposite where we lived. Very often God would speak to me as I watched those sheep fight with one another or wander away from the rest of the flock. Often I would watch the flock all respond to the voice of their master.

A woman who I had gone to India with (we had gone as part of a team), phoned me to say she had heard the word 'Glynn'. When I heard this I had phoned an estate agent in Larne asking for a fully furnished house to rent. Glynn is a small village and to ask specifically for this was a type of madness but, yet again, God had it sorted.

When my first husband and I went to look at it we were very pleased with it. It was a little cottage with an open fire in the living room. In the bathroom there was a jacuzzi in the bath. Every inch of the house oozed character. The landlady was also really pleasant and when we mentioned a security deposit she wouldn't hear of it. She also said we could move in at the weekend! We were stunned.

As we walked away from the house a little car pulled up and it was one of our good friends from the church. She said, 'Have you just been to see a house?' We were amazed how she knew. Basically, she was the cousin of the landlady and when the landlady had phoned her to ask what we were like as people, our friend had highly recommended us, knowing how we had looked after the church as caretakers.

In the background God had worked on our behalf to make sure we had a comfortable home in the middle of a challenging situation. At this stage we were so glad we had obeyed his voice to get rid of our larger items. One of the landlady's stipulations was that whoever was going to rent her home must have no large belongings. My dear friend, your heavenly Father longs for you to seek out his voice, to fellowship with him in such an intimate way. He actually grieves for those who think it was only for Moses or Elijah to hear his voice! He longs to communicate important life messages to you about his love, compassion and provision.

So, there I was enjoying a walk in my new-found place to live. I had ventured down the road, crossing over to find a little bridge. A path ran beside a river that meandered its way through a variety of trees. As I walked along the path I was reminded of Psalm 23. He leads me beside still waters, he restores my soul. If there was ever a time that I needed my soul restored, it was now. Only those who have travelled a severe broken spiritual connection with others who are like family will understand what I mean. It leaves a deep wound that only HE can heal.

As I walked along I noticed two paths. I was drawn to the narrow path. As I walked along this it grew narrower and narrower. At one point I turned and saw a little church. I felt the Holy Spirit say, 'I will show you the church from a different perspective. Not many choose this path.' As time went by I came to understand that God does not see a church with walls or even buildings. He sees people. And when they meet, they are to be led by a multi-leadership. In this there is safety and divine order. When churches are run by one man then beware, as we can even enter into idolatry as everyone hangs on the words of that one person. Not only is this dangerous for us, but it is dangerous for them. Deep insecurity in a leader also works itself out in the form of control and manipulation. A good leader will never feel the need to control as they are secure in their mandate from God.

After Jesus was baptised he went out into the wilderness. He lacked food and water yet yearned for the fellowship of his Father. Wilderness walks are simply us finding our way in a time of dryness. For me, I wasn't at a church. There was nowhere at that time that God was leading us to, because sometimes he will lead you into the wilderness to feed on him. Sometimes we just need answers that no place with walls can give us. It is in these times that we truly find out what we are made of. For me it is where the rubber hits the road. If all you had was Jesus, would he be enough? I believe we are entering days when he will need to be.

Wilderness walks are also defying Satan. As Jesus walked the dusty plains Satan saw the opportunity to kick him when he was weak. All the temptations can fall under idolatry. It is simply the things that we can place BEFORE Almighty God:

- That which we think nourishes us – food, friends, spouse, even church – rather than that which proceeds from God's mouth. His *rhema* and *logos* word: *rhema* is the word he speaks to you NOW; *logos* is the Holy Word (inspired) of God – the Bible.
- To doubt ourselves and think that we are of no use to God's kingdom, in some cases to a point of taking our lives, rather than seeing who we are in God and fulfilling our destinies.
- That we would put anything before God, even ministry, thinking it will fulfil us, rather than worshipping HIM with everything we have.

Jesus was tempted in three ways, yet knew exactly what to say to Satan. Satan offered him food, a way out of his present circumstance and some earthly kingdoms. Jesus simply said NO!

Satan only offered temporal solutions, but Jesus came from a kingdom that was eternal and everlasting. There are things that this earth, or that which roams about the earth, can offer us when we are heavenly bound, but they will never give us lasting peace or divine satisfaction.

We must understand that anything that Satan offers will always pander to either our fleshly appetite or our ego. He offers nothing else because this is why he was thrust out of heaven. He was once an angel in the heavenly place who unfortunately carried wrong motives and managed a mutiny against God. Father God of course threw him out. If we understand this then we can fight against him better, understanding his carnal nature and how he works.

Very often it is those with wrong motives who will give you the most bother in this life as, without even knowing it, they can be used of Satan to attempt ruin in the lives of God's children.

God of course will have the final word in these end times when the motive of every man, woman and child will be laid bare before him. Until then we can settle in our hearts to worship him alone and not let anything else take position in our hearts above him.

Times of wilderness therefore are not to be feared, rather embraced as they can teach us a lot about ourselves and what we truly believe about ourselves and God. If you are in a wilderness now, use it as a time to get to know God better and enter into a deeper understanding of who he is.

Below are some of the attributes I have encountered. I would like to think in ten years' time I will add more to my list. Use the list to identify any you feel you are not aware of and ask the Holy Spirit to reveal those characteristics to you.

The Attributes of the Trinity

Father Heart, Wisdom, Infinitely full of Knowledge, Power, Creator and Creative, Full of Love, Compassion, Kindness, Thoughtfulness, Provider, Protector, Brother, Guide, Comforter, Healer and Lover of my Soul, Deliverer, Saviour, Holy, Sacrificial, Mediator, the Gardener and the Garden, the House Visitor, the Guest at our table, the Risen One, the King of Kings and Lord of Lords, the Lamb and the Lion, the End-Time Warrior whose end-time government will rest on his shoulders (the Alpha and the Omega).

Chapter Five
PART A
Ministry to the Poor and All Things to All Men

*But the Spirit produces love, joy, peace, patience, **kindness**, goodness, faithfulness, humility and self-control.*
Galatians 5:22-23 (GNT)

1972, 2001, 2009, 2013

I watched him walk into the Baptist Hall. I was about eight years old and he looked very dishevelled, his clothes not washed for weeks and he had a long beard. I watched as he looked longingly at the sack of presents as children received their little gifts from Santa.

Something told me that he wanted a gift. Why did no-one give him one? I watched as people from the church looked upon him with disdain. He didn't fit into their world and his presence made them feel uncomfortable.

I will never forget that man. In fact, he is the reason why I went on to run different homeless ministries on the streets of Belfast over the years. 'Out of Darkness' was my first opportunity to live out the passion I had for the homeless. Thankfully I had a very understanding pastor who believed that if you had a desire in your heart to help others, it was placed there by God. I thank God for such men of God who release you into your calling in Christ regardless of your gender or background.

In 2001 I worked as a youth worker in a youth club on the Antrim coast certain evenings of the week. My brother had got me involved and I am thankful to him for this. Young people would help me with the sandwiches, tea and coffee, then I would head to my church in

Jordanstown where sometimes ten other people would join me to venture down on to the streets of Belfast at around eleven o'clock on a Friday night.

We all had the same thing in common: we all had a desire to help those who had found themselves destitute on the streets of Belfast. We would carry down food, tea and coffee and seek to build relationships with people sleeping rough, often cold, lonely and hungry.

God had given me a remit for every group. We were not to mention God to anyone we met. We were to wait until they brought God up in conversation. The person was to be fed and watered and, most importantly, we were to sit down beside a person and talk eye to eye, not stand over them. Basically, this was a love ministry.

Often, as we did the above, tears would appear on a person's cheek. They were not used to people treating them with kindness or speaking to them as a human being. Sometimes a person would ask, 'Why are you doing this?' That gave opportunity then to speak of God's heart for the people he loved.

It was in the first group I pioneered that we met a middle-aged man and he was truly a character. I will call him Frank. He believed in God and would at times speak of God as if at one time in his life he had given his life to him, only to later lose his way. When we met Frank he was consuming between five and six bottles of wine a day. Over the years Frank would pop up in the various groups.

When I first led a team on to the streets of Belfast I never dreamt that I would end up homeless myself. After ten years of my first marriage I found myself in a women's aid hostel in Belfast, understanding hostel life first hand. This would only deepen my understanding of destitution and a dependence on God.

My first hostel experience taught me that there are people struggling behind closed doors. Not all homeless are on the street. Many are in hostels or sofa-surfing amongst friends. All have one thing in common: they don't have a home they can call their own.

In some of these times my guitar would help me through and songs I wrote would lift up my soul to God. One song I wrote in these times was called 'Mighty Deliverer'. I have included it for the words as obviously it's not quite the same if you can't hear it. Someday I will record some songs written from my difficult places, until then I hope the words will lift others in similar circumstances.

MIGHTY DELIVERER

Holy, Mighty Deliverer, yeah, Mighty One
Holy, Mighty Deliverer, yeah Holy, Mighty One

He lifts us up from a dark, dark pit
He lifts us up from deep despair
He makes a way where there seems to be no way
Reveals himself and shows that he is there

Holy, Mighty Deliverer, yeah Holy, Mighty One
Holy, Mighty Deliverer, Holy, Mighty One
Mighty One, Mighty One

He gives us streams of water in the wilderness
He gives us cloud by day and gives us fire by night

He gives us manna, Jesus, for our daily bread
He gives us angels so we need not fear where we tread

Holy, Mighty Deliverer, Holy Mighty One
Holy, Mighty Deliverer, Holy, Mighty One, Mighty One, Mighty One
(Copyright © 2008 Naomi Smyth)

'Hope to Help' was a different ministry in years to come. Leading up to it, I had a stint of homelessness. This time it related to taking a woman into my home. Unfortunately, it didn't turn out too well and sometimes I couldn't get into my own house, even though I was the one who rented the three-bedroom house. Eventually, I stayed at the top part of where I worked and pulled the lease on the house. In the midst of helping another I didn't think I would need to go to such extremes but I felt that I was in a very controlling situation.

At around this time I was helped by a couple in the new-found church I went to and they put me up for a short time before God opened the door for me to have a bedsit of my own.

It was in this time that the senior pastor challenged us to use what was in our hands for the kingdom of God. For me, I felt that in the past I had run a homeless ministry. I spoke to senior leadership who travelled frequently to encourage us in the Belfast church.

When a leader heard what I wanted to do, he was a great encouragement to me and said that if I ever had anyone who wanted rehabilitation then he would pay for the transport for them to get to Bradford and be helped by a man who ran a ministry to help addicts. This man had been homeless for many years on the streets of Dublin and now ran various ministries to help those who found themselves in the same position. He had set up various rehab units across the country and the leader suggested if anyone in Belfast needed rehab that this could be facilitated through this man's ministry.

Within weeks of the leader giving me this wonderful offer I had started 'Hope to Help' and bumped into Frank again. This time he was very broken and cried out for help. When I suggested the rehab in Bradford he jumped at the chance. It meant me taking two days off work as Frank didn't have identification so this meant we had to go via the boat route.

The money was organised and given to me to take Frank over to meet the man who ran the ministries. It was a ten-hour journey.

I will never forget us going through the scanners at P&O Ferries and the woman handing me a bottle of wine that Frank was trying to sneak through. He was over the limit! I carried it in my bag hoping to pass it on to someone who liked wine who *didn't* have an addiction issue.

Later I would see that same bottle up on the stage of the church in Bradford as a female pastor shared how it had been passed to her from the hands of a homeless man. When I had safely left Frank with the man who ran the rehab ministries, I met with the pastor and asked him if either he or his wife drank wine. He had taken it home and I think his wife was amused by the gift. The team back in Belfast also found it amusing as that particular service was televised back in Belfast.

I had a generous invite from the man who ran the ministries and his wife to join them for dinner before returning the next day to Belfast. That was an enjoyable evening. I met with other couples who had all prayed, asking God for ideal partners. They said, 'Write a list.' I took their advice and wrote a list.

The next day I made it back to Belfast. That evening I headed out on the streets of Belfast as this was a 'Hope to Help' night. To my shock I saw Frank sitting at Botanic Gardens train station. Sophie, another team member, went across to speak with him as she could see I was angry. In weeks to come I would speak to him again, when I had calmed down, and he would banter me and I would banter him. That night he told Sophie that he had no proper contact with family in Bradford. The man who ran the ministries told me later that he had been very firm with Frank when he wanted to return home. He told him from his own experience that he would not have long to live if he kept travelling down his chosen path. In 2010 Frank was found in an alley with heroin pumped into his system. It is still unknown if this was pumped in by Frank (as his vice was drink) or someone else, but the reality was he died a horrible death. Sometimes we are unable to help others as they are determined to walk on a path of their choosing.

Choice is a gift from God. We may not view it as such, but it has been this way since the Garden. Addiction is a very powerful force, but the Holy Spirit is more powerful. If we surrender ourselves to the Holy Spirit, we can overcome addictions.

'Hope to Help' moved from strength to strength and I thank God for the people that God placed beside me. Because it was a love ministry and at one point there were twelve team members, I was struck by the resemblance of the twelve disciples.

I had one very young 'Timothy' by my side. (If you read the book of Timothy you will take my point that sometimes youths are not always encouraged the way they should be, when in fact they can bring so much to a team.) In my case this Timothy was my 'John' (the disciple who loved Jesus and kept very close). He remained very close to me and seemed determined to learn all he could to help the homeless. It does not surprise me that this young man went on to do thirteen-hour shifts in a homeless shelter and then move into politics, dealing especially with social issues.

Another young woman had the gift of sitting with a homeless person as if she was in their living room. She had a love and a compassion that was so necessary for this ministry. She also had parents who published, so when it came to doing a 'Gig in the Park' in Botanic Gardens, she would provide beautiful literature for passers-by as artists sang songs of hope, businesses gave away free food and face-painters from the church gave a free service to eager children. We also had the director of a resource company give free security barriers, security men and offered any help he could. This link had come through one of our team who worked in a governmental building. Once the word got out that we were helping the homeless, the director of the company had offered his help. God had snow-balled this ministry because it was his heart to help people in trouble.

Many gifts were used that day. It had been a long journey for me also as I had approached the council months previously and carried out risk assessments and met with all their requirements.

This special day was to raise awareness for those who faced homelessness. Another young woman was a photographer and she had produced photographs using some of our own team to picture a person in a sleeping bag, in a hoody, face hidden. They were very powerful images.

Another young man presented the event on the stage as he also presented in the church. Like I said, gifts galore. What was beautiful about this for me was the fact that all these gifts lay within each person. It always blessed me so much to see people move into their gifts and flourish in them. I have yet to see the same again since

'Hope to Help'. I feel honoured that God allowed me to head-up such a beautiful bunch of people.

I have written of these two groups to highlight our need to follow in Christ's footsteps. I also had people from the churches back home praying. For me these precious people were just as valuable as those on the streets. Where are we without prayer support and praying every step through with the Almighty?

In the Gospels we read that Jesus reached out to those who had felt forgotten or rejected. Nothing has changed and if you want to follow in his footsteps, first invite him into your life, then ask him to show you those who need to be loved. You will be surprised. It isn't just the homeless person sitting on the street corner . . . it could equally be that person sitting with everything materially, but just as lonely and without hope in their mind and soul.

As sons and daughters of the Living God we have a message of good news that our God is a God of hope. No situation is beyond him. If you feel you have fallen too far from his grace, he is waiting with open arms, like the father of the prodigal son. Of course God cares if you squander time, resources or money, but even if you have done this and make your way back to him, he will only throw you a party! He will not reject you.

PART B
Leader or Servant?

We watched as the policemen put on their blue gloves to help lift a homeless man off the street. He struggled as he saw the uniforms, possibly thinking he was being arrested. I called on another member of the team and we went over to the man who had fallen back on to the road and lay in dangers way. He responded to us because we looked harmless and hopefully we looked as if we were there to help. He took our arms and we safely set him on the footpath beside a wall. We offered him tea or coffee and a freshly made sandwich.

He looked at us incredulously, wondering why on earth we were helping him. We sat down beside him, giving him opportunity to share his world with us, his struggles and his life of destitution. Beyond the hot drink we offered socks, toothbrush, toothpaste, soap and clothes, as very often the homeless struggle to keep themselves clean on the streets.

Earlier that night I filled the flasks for the hot tea and coffee. Why? Because I understood a certain kingdom principle. In order to be a leader you must first be a servant. I sometimes saw a look or a comment from either team members or rough sleepers that said, 'Why are you doing this?' I often thought of Jesus washing his disciples' feet. Peter too had the same incredulous look on his face when Jesus went to wash his feet. In John 13:7-9 Jesus said, 'You do not realise now what I am doing, but later you will understand.' Peter's answer is one of total misunderstanding. Peter said, 'You shall never wash my feet.' When Jesus says, 'Unless I wash you, you have no part with me', Peter answers, 'Then, Lord, not just my feet but my hands and my head as well.'

I think of the complexity of this. Not only are we being told that being a leader means being a servant first, but it also speaks of the cleansing that Jesus will bring to us through the Holy Spirit . . . if we let him.

For me, being a leader was not about telling people what to do or lording anything over anyone. It was simply an opportunity to serve my master and help others to do the same.

One thing I believe Jesus was always showing us in the Gospels (Matthew, Mark, Luke and John): he was continually being an example because he understood that we need visuals in order to learn.

In Israel at the time that Jesus washed his disciples' feet, it was part of their custom for travellers to have the dust washed off their feet before a communal meal. Traditionally the lowest of servants would carry out this task. When Jesus did what he did, he was making it clear that in the kingdom of God there was no room for ego or position playing. Jesus would have a similar conversation with his disciples when they argued as to who was the greatest. In Luke 22:26 Jesus says, 'Let him who is the greatest among you become like the youngest, and him who is the chief and leader like one who serves' (AMPC).

Therefore, serving should be at the forefront of your daily walk and ministry. If you ever think that an action is beneath you then you have missed something very profound in God's kingdom. To serve another is another opportunity to serve the King of kings. The purest acts are those done in private. If we do kind acts to another and we are seen then we have our thanks on this earth, but what we do in private to bless another, this will always bless the Father's heart more as we have not done it to attain man's approval or to be seen to be good.

When the homeless ministry we ran made it into the local paper for our 'good works', part of me cringed. Only God saw my heart as I never pioneered any of the work on the streets to receive worldly acclaim. For me it was a call in the deepest part of my heart, from the age of eight when I saw the loneliness in the homeless man who entered our little church hall.

Please don't misunderstand me. I am not a special person or a person of much acclaim. Later in this book you will read of a vision that was given to me by God himself. May I make this very clear: God does not give dreams or visions to anyone because they are special. When I look back at my life I feel that God gave me visions and dreams because that is the only way I heard him or grasped what he was saying. He created me to receive this way. In fact, I have joked with people and said it is for the hard of hearing that God gives visions and dreams.

When I think of Paul, I know he had the same problem as me. In his case he had to be blinded on the road to Damascus in order to get what God was saying. After he had his powerful experience he was never the same. The same man who had persecuted other Christians, was now one himself! He would go on to share revelation after revelation of Jesus.

Paul was the one apostle who didn't have first-hand experience of walking with Jesus when he was on this earth like the other disciples did, yet he understood Christ and his principles like someone who did walk with the Saviour. Simply this was down to revelation.

We all have the opportunity to do the same. We do not have to walk face to face with Jesus in order to receive revelation of who he is. If we allow the Holy Spirit to come into our lives and change us then we can experience Jesus the same way that the apostle Paul did.

Interestingly, we find Paul, who was considered to be one of the greatest apostles, describe himself as 'the least of the apostles' (1 Corinthians 15:9). I believe that Paul understood servitude and is an example to us all.

Finally, position our eyes on Jesus who quite simply is the greatest example of what a servant is . . . after all, he laid down his life for every one of us. May we, in turn, lay down our lives.

All Things to All Men

1996, 2000

Earlier in this book I mentioned a little cottage in the village of Glynn, Northern Ireland. It was from here that I travelled half way across the world to experience my first mission trip, and that was to India.

My first husband was the only one of us who was earning at this time, yet God still made it clear that I was going to Chennai, Madras, with a team of seven others from Northern Ireland.

Before we left the church in Larne I had attended a women's day. I had heard of the trip to India and had asked God to show me if I was to go. There was a need for women to teach sewing skills and to travel with a team across to Chennai, Madras, so that young women would not venture back into prostitution. In my heart I wanted to go but I needed confirmation.

In the conference I heard the gentle whisper of the Holy Spirit asking me to kneel. I remember saying back to the Holy Spirit, 'What, in front of all these people?' The Holy Spirit was persistent. Everyone was standing so it was really obvious when I dropped to my knees! The next thing I knew there was a woman pointing at me from across the room. She said, 'I had a vision and I have just seen that woman in a sari.' I was stunned. I do love it, though, when God confirms what he has spoken into your heart.

So, leading up to going on my first mission trip I received a lesson in Jehovah Jireh – 'The Lord is my Provider'.

God had made it clear that he was going to provide all of the money needed for the trip. He spoke into my spirit one day communicating that if I worked for a company and the boss said he would pay my way, I would believe him. He communicated that HE was my boss! And that the company would pay for it. As the months rolled on that is exactly what happened. The company of people I was going with all got nudges to pay various parts of my trip.

Just before going on the trip I had a stubborn moment and insisted on getting £60 in travellers' cheques. I remember God communicating to my spirit that he would match it.

At the airport I met with the other team members and to my shock one of them took me to one side and told me how she had received a nudge from God to do a car-boot sale. She said, 'I had £50 for you and then a woman walked up and bought three coats, so there is £60 for you for the trip.' Amazing . . . isn't God just wonderful. He never ceases to blow me away with his intricate plans, often behind the scenes.

The night we arrived in India, it was late. The lady who ran the ministry in India met us at the airport. The bright garland flowers were gently placed around our shoulders. Their culture was to honour their guests and with such a beautiful gesture. We drove past people lying on the streets, destitute, yet in amongst the extreme poverty was extreme beauty. I watched as women dressed in brightly coloured saris disappeared into little huts. They looked so beautifully dressed; it was unexpected to see them live in such poverty.

Even in those late hours little yellow taxis whizzed past. There were almost no signs or traffic lights, and animals wandered around aimlessly as if they owned the road. Later I was to find out they practically did own the streets as they are considered sacred by the nation.

The lady who ran the ministry in India introduced herself. She had married into the Brahmin caste, which was considered the highest caste in India. Originally a politician until she became a Christian not long after her husband had died, now God used her to help prostitutes, orphans and widows. She had her own slot on Indian television and she even had entry into the brothels in Mumbai. She used her position to run a home for 130 children. This woman, to be honest, was one of the strongest Christian women that I would meet in my early Christian years. It took guts to do what she had accomplished.

Four of us had agreed to stay at this lady's house. The other four stayed in a hotel. For me I enjoyed staying amongst the people of the country that I was travelling to. I learnt more about how they lived and their culture. Also, on that mission trip I learnt that God was doing a multi- bless.

If you travel with the mindset that you are going to bless another nation, then that's fine. But it is a bit arrogant! In mission you learn a lot and you come back home humbled by another way of life and also God blesses you! That's the way God works. Yes, he appreciates your heart to bless others, but God is always thinking about his co-workers, looking to bless everyone in individual and collective ways.

Little children gave their best performance as they danced for us. God had also put a dance on my heart for them. It was called 'The Cross of Silence' and it had Indian-style music. It portrayed Jesus' painful walk to crucifixion. God had led me to the music in a library. It was in fact an 'All Things to All Men' moment as God put into my hands music that these beautiful Indian people could relate to yet appreciate the visual of dance to see Christ's sacrifice and struggle.

We also had a moment of speaking to thousands of people at an outside church. The men wore white and the women had scarves on their heads. When we looked out, the sight was that of which I had seen in a dream. In the dream the fields were white with a harvest of souls. God spoke to me that day. It was a harvest of souls into his kingdom, thousands of souls. The dream had come to pass.

We took a trip outside the city to faraway villages. On a piece of land, we prayed and took communion with the woman who ran the ministry in India. Later, this land would be secured for her and her many children. It took provision and many battles, but God provided for her and her children, the way he had provided for me.

Very often God is teaching us to trust him, and as we floated out in a boat on Indian waters to experience the breath-taking views, we all thought of Peter stepping out of the boat in trust of his Saviour's words and we all felt the call to be fishers of men on that boat and the cost involved.

The most poignant moment for me on the whole trip was when we visited St Thomas Mount. This is where the apostle Thomas had brought Christianity to the Indian people. Thomas had managed to share Christianity with the Brahmin people first. This wasn't because they were a more superior people, but simply it was because he wanted all walks of life to know the wonderful news that Christ had died for them personally. Unfortunately, when Thomas had ventured out to share the good news of Christianity to other castes, they didn't like it and someone took a knife and stabbed Thomas in the back and killed him. This was how Thomas had died. Ironically, my dance had included Thomas in it – his doubting. Yet to any Christian in India, Thomas held a special place in their heart. Even though he had been known as 'the Doubter', his final moments were given in sacrifice for his Lord and Saviour, Jesus.

'All Things to All Men' would play out in my life again when I had the opportunity to visit Uganda.

Two men had stayed in our house in Carrickfergus back in 1999. One was Korean and one was Ugandan. A friend had asked us to put up two men who were over to pray for Ireland. The Ugandan had asked us to go to Uganda, to meet the children that he looked after. He also ran an orphanage.

By 2000 I had met a woman called Sarah in an inner-healing conference in Minneapolis. Sarah was from Texas and was planning to travel to Ireland to trace her ancestors. I offered for her to stay at our house and she was delighted to have such an offer.

Within three months Sarah came to Ireland and our friendship was cemented as she visited different aspects in my life, from 'Out of Darkness' homeless ministry to the drop-in centre for youth in Whitehead. We showed Sarah the beautiful sights that Northern Ireland possesses, from the Giant's Causeway to the Glens of Antrim. Sarah also invited us to Midland, Texas, so we spent twelve days with her family on a 'buy one get one free' airplane ticket offer that *The Belfast Telegraph* newspaper did at that time (provision, yet again!).

I had told Sarah of my visit to Uganda and she was interested, but it would take my first husband to drop out in the months leading up to the planned trip for Sarah to suggest that she also went. I was delighted to have her join me. I met her in London and we travelled to Uganda together. It was on this trip that Sarah met her future husband.

Sarah would marry, live in Kampala, Uganda, for a short time and then travel to Texas. It took time for her husband to get a visa. In years to come they set up a vocational school in Kampala that would bless many. Vocational skills were taught to train up men and women in skills so that they could set up their own businesses.

I travelled back in 2015 to see how the vocational school was going and then in 2017 to visit the school once more and watch a graduation service. Back home, with the help of some friends we had raised some money to help the students once they passed through the school.

I also had the pleasure of seeing Ruthie's introduction in 2018. In Uganda, introduction is like a huge engagement party where both families meet before marriage. Ruthie had been about fourteen when I first visited Uganda and she had worked as a maid in the Ugandan man's house when I visited in 2000. We had struck up a friendship and I had never forgotten her. Now she was marrying and she had asked my friend and I to be part of her ceremony. So in the trip of 2018, they dressed us in the *gomesi*, which is a little bit Star Trekky with pointy shoulders. They asked us to move in dance as we followed the party of women who danced before their future husbands' families. I think I possibly moved my hips too much as the crowd laughed until they could laugh no more at our interpretation of their music and culture, and when an African gentleman said to me, 'I think you are black on the inside', I reckoned I had some decent rhythm!

We also visited an outer village to see where Sarah's husband's father lived. When we visited his father there was an albino girl there. His story of how the albino child was born was very interesting. My friend Sarah had visited and her mother-in-law had criticised Sarah. Not long after this, his wife had given birth to an albino child. The father had told his wife that she had a white baby because of her attitude towards Sarah. The story was extraordinary but had always stuck with me. Because of the circumstances they had called the girl Sarah. I watched as she went out into the sun and came back in within a short time sunburnt. The father told us how they had become part of an albino society. They would collect sunglasses and suntan lotion to provide for those who were albinos. Albinos suffered greatly in Uganda. Sometimes they were killed as surrounding people thought that their white skin meant they were blessed financially. They would literally kill them for their skin.

In my heart in 2016 I had spoken a simple prayer to God: 'Let me bring suntan lotions and sun glasses back the next time for these people.' In 2017 a friend of mine was having a 'skip hoke' in Belfast (things thrown out by others and considered as rubbish). He found bags and bags of suntan lotions. He messaged me to say he was going to put them on eBay. I said, 'No, I know who they are for!' Shirley and I carried them across in our luggage and it was with great pleasure that I left them on a little table for Sarah's father-in-law, as well as sun glasses I had picked up in every charity shop I had been in for two years.

I had bought a set of bathroom scales for weighing our cases. Ironically, the caption on the packaging read, 'She believed she could, so she did.' No doubt this was about losing weight, but for me it was about believing that we could carry so much weight to Uganda.

Not only were there items for the albinos, but also for a church in the ghetto. I had struck up a friendship with a rapping pastor who came from the ghetto. His life had been transformed. Now he led a church in one of the ghetto areas of Kampala.

We also carried across packs for ex-addicts that contained a facecloth, soap, toothbrush, toothpaste, a little bar of chocolate and a card with a spiritual message.

Again, I saw the provision of God as the airline had a special deal on 28kg of baggage each plus 8kg to carry on board. Altogether we could carry 72kg. What a blessing!

If there is one thing that meeting Sarah had taught me it is this: never underestimate the power of connection. I had met Sarah in a toilet in Minneapolis. When I heard she was coming to Ireland I invited her into my home. Never miss the windows of opportunity that God places before you. You just never know what God will bring out of those connections. They can literally change your life and the lives of others. God is waiting to bless you and allow that blessing to ripple out and touch a multitude. Be ready and keep your eyes and ears open. Watch with a giving heart and he will bless you beyond your wildest dreams. He is asking every one of us to be all things to all men. Amen.

Chapter Six
Nowhere to Lay My Head

*But the Spirit produces love, joy, peace, patience, kindness, **goodness**, faithfulness, humility and self-control.*
Galatians 5:22-23 (GNT)

Summer 2004

In this chapter I will allude to times that I had nowhere to lay my head. So there I was . . . Down South. My first husband and I had moved down from the north after selling our house in Carrickfergus. I had taken a chance, saying to my husband, 'If you manhandle me again I will leave.'

We had married in 1994. I had seen him as a highly spiritual man. In hindsight I know he had spiritual qualities; he just lacked qualities in the husband department. If you have never been married before you can think certain behaviour is normal, like silences or control draped in gestures of love.

Let me make something very clear in this chapter of my life. Whether someone puts you down, hurts you emotionally, mentally, physically, sexually or even spiritually . . . it is all abuse. In my case, my first husband manhandled me and operated in control.

Some will not understand why a woman stays in such a relationship. There can be many reasons. Firstly, abuse can be a familiar friend. If you don't know anything else or have low self-worth, you will never see yourself deserving a pure love. It also takes certain strength to leave. Sometimes something has to snap in order to go a different way and walk a different path.

I had given my marriage one last chance. At first, when we moved down south to a house in County Carlow, it seemed idealist, with chickens and a piece of ground, but soon we were moving to a small cottage further into County Wicklow and the abuse started again, with him pushing me towards the ground.

My first husband helped me pack my car. I guess he knew that he had stepped over the mark and he had broken his word. I left at eight o'clock at night with a duvet, two plates, two knives and forks, some CDs and a few items. I didn't know where I was going, I just needed to 'get out'.

I had nowhere to lay my head . . . but I had my heavenly Father and he would direct me over the next few days, where to go and where to stay. Even on the motorway there was a big cross all lit up along the way. That cross really comforted me.

My first port of call was a friend I had gone to India with on a mission trip. In fact, three members of the India team would all play their part as I spent one night here and one night there. Eventually, I had exhausted my short stays with everyone. I remember standing on a pier not knowing which way to turn. I remember clearly the devil beckoning me to walk down a set of steps into the water. I whispered to him, 'I am not my own but Christ's . . . therefore you can't have me.' I turned 180 degrees and looked . . . there was a lighthouse. For me, when I had turned there was a visual of Jesus. He will always shine a light on our dark path.

Soon I received a phone call from one of the women from the India trip. She suggested going to a women's aid hostel. I phoned and they took me in straight away. They were amazing and I lay my head down on a pillow and had the best night's sleep I'd had for a very long time.

So, temporarily, I knew what it was to not have anywhere to lay my head. Jesus knew this constantly. The experience taught me to be grateful for the small things we have in life.

Very soon I was working part time from the hostel and we even had a hostel move to new premises. The housing executive found me a flat in Sandy Row as I attended a church in Sandy Row.

So, that had been my first experience of homelessness, where my car had been vital for getting from the south to the north of Ireland. At one point I thought that I would sleep in my car. I was prepared to, but God intervened.

Other times I would experience homelessness, times of unchosen circumstances. Every time came the same revelation: Jesus was there to carry me, to comfort me and to guide me.

Maybe your 'nowhere to lay my head' is insomnia. I never suffered this until I had circumstances in my life where sleep evaded me. Even in menopause we can suffer insomnia. This is definitely a type of 'not being able to lay our heads down'. Sometimes we can use these times to pray. There is nothing better than seeking God's face at three in the morning! At first we can feel tired, but then as we receive revelation and peace for difficult situations, God very often gives his heavenly perspective and turns all negative things in our life to the positive, if we let him.

'Heavenly Father, when we find ourselves bereft of sleep, regardless of circumstances, help us to turn to you and seek your face. May we stay awake in times of kingdom need. May we discern the seasons, when you need us to push through for your kingdom's sake. Amen.'

Chapter Seven
Betrayal

*But the Spirit produces **love**, joy, peace, patience, kindness, goodness,*
faithfulness, humility and self-control.
Galatians 5:22-23 (GNT)

This chapter has possibly been the hardest to write. Betrayal is never something we experience from those we don't know but rather it is the people closest to us.

For Jesus, his betrayal would come from the one in the group who kept the money, therefore he was trusted. It also needs to be noted that Satan entered Judas in order to betray Jesus because it was destined that Jesus would die for the sins of the world. God always has a greater purpose in the sorrows we endure in this life. Yet when betrayal strikes it usually cuts to our very heart and it is very hard for us to see a divine purpose that God is working in the midst of devastation.

I remember God showing me that to the degree that any Christian is surrendered to Christ, let's say 80 per cent, then what's left is an open door for Satan to work through.

Remember Jesus' words to Peter when Peter thought that Jesus didn't really need to die. Jesus says, 'Get behind me, Satan' (Matthew 16:23). These words can shock us as we think that Peter was only making a suggestion and had Jesus' best interests at heart. But if Peter had been fully surrendered to Christ he would have known that Jesus carried a great responsibility regarding his heavenly purpose and that he had to die so that we could have eternal life. Basically, Father God had a redemptive plan and it wasn't an option for Jesus not to go to the cross.

When betrayal happened to me, I have to be honest and say that it took me ages to properly forgive. For me it is not about writing the detail of those betrayals in this book; it is all about forgiveness. As Jesus hung on the cross he uttered these words that are extremely profound: 'Father, forgive them, for they do not know what they are doing' (Luke 23:34).

These words have been priceless for me. I have taken these words so many times and applied them to my life again and again to painful situations. I can honestly say, hand on heart, that people don't know how they are hurting you. They seriously don't have a clue!

One day God said to me, 'Your perspective and your sister's in Christ are two different perspectives as to what happened in those painful months.' He reminded me of a third perspective . . . his!

Have you ever questioned an argument between two children? There is a lot of 'He said', 'She said', and so it can be with us. We are the children of God and we can focus on what the other person said. Don't get me wrong, there can be situations that God calls you out of that he is not asking you to be in, but if he does this, then he is certainly asking you to practise forgiveness for the ways in which you were wronged.

Rarely do people actually mean to betray or hurt us, and those that do are very often caught in a destructive cycle that has carried on for generation after generation until someone breaks the cycle.

Even Judas regretted his actions after he had carried them out. When words are spoken they cannot be put back into our mouths.

As others betray us, we can then equally betray others. If we think we are free of getting it wrong then we are saying we are free from sin . . . and none of us are sinless.

So I chose to forgive those who have transgressed against me. I had decided to watch a film. I was struck by so many parallels even in my own life. There was a character in the film who got to know the Trinity The character is asked to forgive the one who abducts, abuses and kills his little daughter. As he carries her limp body down from the mountain he repeats over and over again, 'I forgive you, I forgive you, and I forgive you.' When I watched that part of the film I sobbed as I thought of my own journey and forgiving those who had hurt me even though I didn't 'feel' like it.

I also understand that just because we forgive people, especially in church situations, it doesn't mean that things will change magically for us. Often God can lift us out of situations to start afresh and to be amongst a people who will love and respect us, and we them. In an ideal world we could stay and everything would be fine, but I guess God loves us and knows what is best for us. Equally, he can ask us to stay, to forgive and move in the midst of a less than perfect situation.

The second part of the forgiveness learning curve for me was a time when I felt that others had hurt me but that they knew exactly what they were doing. I found this one much harder and had to gain a heavenly perspective. If you ever find it hard to forgive and you truly want to follow Jesus . . . always ask the Holy Spirit for divine perspective. There are times in our own human-ness that we struggle more than we should, but heavenly perspective always helps.

So, one day I was struggling. Father God reiterated that HE was and is the Great I AM and that HE lives on the inside of me. He then directed me to the Roman solider who tortured Christ and he said, 'He didn't truly KNOW who he was. When others hurt you deliberately, they don't know who you are – or they wouldn't even dare.' In other words, if people truly had a fear of God they wouldn't dream of doing half the things they do to us.

There was a second element to this. Jesus was silent. I thought about that and meditated on it. Jesus didn't hang from the cross saying, 'Do you not realise who I am?' He could have, but he didn't. He was silent to the mocking and the scorn.

This really, really helped me, simply because I struggled with others' motives when they hurt me, especially if it appeared that it was a deliberate act. This explanation helped me to release those who did things unaware of what they were actually doing. On that day in the future, at the judgement seat of Christ, he will show us all how we have fallen short and there will be much weeping, but then he will wipe away every tear. I believe whoever is left in those days, we will receive a mighty revelation about forgiveness. Much better that we learn it now and that we don't hold back on what Christ wants to do in these last days. If we choose to lie and lick our wounds, we lose valuable time that can be spent for the kingdom. Therefore I implore you . . . whatever the betrayal, whatever the hurt, forgive it and allow Jesus to pour oil on your wounds.

Otherwise, unforgiveness can rattle around your body like a poison. It can actually make you ill. Unforgiveness can twist your soul.

If you feel you want to forgive but have struggled, God knows your heart.

'Father God, you know how much I want to follow you and I know that means letting go of the things that have happened that can hinder me in my walk. Today I choose to forgive and I ask for your divine forgiveness to flood my being out to those who have hurt me, either knowingly or unknowingly. Bless their lives, Lord. Fill my soul with your undeniable love and grace. Amen.'

Chapter Eight
Crucifixion

*But the Spirit produces love, joy, peace, patience, kindness, goodness, faithfulness, humility and **self-control**.*
Galatians 5:22-23 (GNT)

When I was thinking of this chapter I thought of how we are called to die to our own desires. Firstly, though, God asked me to share this vision as I believe it is to help others.

This vision was given to me at a time when I was struggling to forgive myself for something I had done wrong. When we become a Christian we can struggle when we first sin. This can partly be because we are led to believe that God turns his face away from us.

In the vision Jesus was on the cross. He was passing through crucifixion. The view was taken from an 'above' perspective, as if from a helicopter. I came to understand it was what Father God saw from heaven as his Son suffered a horrific death. He watched as his Son was brutally murdered and hung on those bits of wood. Father God said this to me: 'I NEVER took my eyes off my Son the whole time.' I remember thinking about all the times in church I had heard the words 'And he turned away from his Son because the sin of the world was on him.'

So I had a conversation with Father God and, to cut a long story short, Father God said that if he turned his face away every time someone sinned, he would never look on mankind.

We have a Big God who is big enough to look upon the earth and all that has fallen short of his glory. Does he ever tire of mankind and its sin? Yes, absolutely. Does he turn away from his creation as much as is made out? No! Absolutely not.

He gazed upon his Son as he 'took' the sins of the world on his bruised body. He never took his eyes off his beautiful Son.

This means one thing to us sinners when we mess up . . . he doesn't turn his face away. We can come boldly before the throne of grace and receive forgiveness. For anyone who feels deep shame and condemnation to a place where they avoided God . . . you don't have to avoid him anymore. He is waiting with open arms to shine his face upon you. He wishes that his Son's death was not in vain, that all who feel trapped by their sin come to him.

So what is this 'death to self' that we Christians speak of . . . or don't!

For me, in my life, it has always been about two things: SURRENDER and OBEDIENCE.

Simply, God will ask and we must comply, not because we are afraid but out of love. The ultimate 'love act' was completed by Jesus for his Father. We see a similar ask when Abraham was asked to sacrifice his son. Abraham complied. Not only did Abraham comply, but he trusted God enough to sacrifice the promise God had spoken of, which probably didn't make sense. Abraham blindly obeyed.

I experienced this in my life as God asked me to give up my boyfriend and, later, my husband. When God speaks of a union like 'two lovebirds', it's hard when you have to walk away, but God always has a master plan. It's in the dying to your own desires that you allow God to 'do his thing'. Sometimes this can invite others misunderstanding you and wondering all sorts, but within this we can learn not to care what others think. This can kill off any fear of man that may reside in us.

My life has been far from the neat, perfect portrayal of a Christian woman. I have not set out to be this way, but I have found as I have walked and talked with God that he has accepted me in my imperfect ways. He is full of grace. My crucifixion is nowhere near Jesus' crucifixion – firstly, because he is perfect; secondly, because his crucifixion was physically, emotionally and mentally beyond what any of us can imagine.

God will ask us to follow after Christ in ways similar and we must never be afraid to see the correlations. Jesus simply asks for our obedience and trust. As he reaches out his hand in a beckoning manner, we are to obediently arise and say the words found in Isaiah 6:8, 'Here am I. Send me!' It is worth noting that the words 'I am' are in this proclamation. So the Great I AM is within every one of his children. He asks that each I AM rises up and goes forth into this world. Our planet needs to experience 'The Great I AM'. We each have a different experience of the same God, in our lives. Let's share it.

As we crucify our own desires, God will rise up in us like a phoenix. From our death and our ashes springs forth life. This is how it works in the kingdom of God.

No other religion offers us eternal salvation. No other religion offers a spotless lamb, sinless, crucified to bring eternal life to a whole dying world. Yes, certainly there are religions that offer 'works' as an answer to gain spiritual rewards, but it is not by works that we will enter into his kingdom; it is purely by the blood of our Lord Jesus Christ.

'Thank you, Jesus, for sacrificing your life so that we may live and live it to an abundance. May we offer our lives as living sacrifices and follow in your footsteps. Amen.'

Chapter Nine
Raised to New Life

*But the Spirit produces love, **joy**, peace, patience, kindness, goodness, faithfulness, humility and self-control.*

Galatians 5:22-23 (GNT)

22 02 2022

In the beginning, man's first experience of God was in the Garden of Eden. God walked with Adam, and he was truly blessed. As we know, this union was interrupted by Adam and Eve failing to follow the voice of God. 'Do not eat of that tree' (see Genesis 2:17).

The beautiful union was broken, but God implemented his Plan B and used his Son's death to reconcile mankind back to himself. Thousands of years later Jesus would walk in another garden after conquering death and, for all who would accept him, he would redeem generations back to a patient loving Father who sits with open arms waiting for those to return to him.

Jesus is the Christ, the Messiah, the Redeemer, the Saviour and the Lion of Judah.

Recently he also shared with me that he is 'the Garden'.

This is what he revealed . . .

Jesus carries the four seasons in his being. He brings life, he brings joy, he brings colour and provides food. He is the backdrop to every outdoor fellowship, and he gives a home to every animal and bird.

He is in every detail, even beyond the human eye. He is in every sound, every bird song; creation sings his name. He is in the quietness with his still small voice. He is also in the sound of pruning, as all the dead gets cut away, and even that which isn't dead gets cut away to bring forth more life. The Father is the Master Pruner – as Jesus is fully aware as his life was cut down to bring forth more life . . . eternal life.

So, Jesus died so that we could have new life, and have it in abundance. As Christians we can feel that we are not living as full a life as we should. So, what's the key? For me it's in the dying. When we learn to die we then live, and we live a fuller life.

Recently God led me to open house groups. He spoke to me about 'the hungry, the thirsty and those feeling isolated'. Two years had already passed since the pandemic outbreak. Churches had closed and this was truly a time when the faith of many was being tested.

It wasn't too hard to see a time in the future where it would be difficult to buy or sell without some kind of mark. We were in a precursor to the end times. Fellowship was key. I couldn't shake the feeling that God was aligning his church to go back to its basic roots – house church.

It wasn't long before we had two house groups: one in Ballyhalbert and one in Belfast. People were glad of a connection.

We met, ate, sang, prayed and shared different videos and information that had been passed to us individually. We even visited churches that hadn't closed their doors when the pandemic hit.

So our new life is all about living for Jesus, in whatever way he is asking or seeking from us. It is to be a light; to be salt that hasn't lost its flavour. One night, some of us shared what salt meant to us.

Firstly, food without salt is boring. When salt is added it brings out all the flavours. And so Christ is with us. Without him we can be flavourless and boring in this world. Others need to see something different so that they can have relief from their lives as without Christ all our lives are muted.

Salt preserves, as any good butcher will tell you. Rubbed in to 'keep' the meat. God can use us to 'hold back' the evil in this world and preserve what is good and moral.

Salt glistens. Christ can use us to shine and light the way to a lost and dying world. Anything that is like a diamond carries a facet. This speaks of all the many attributes of the Trinity. We too should shine and show a dying world all the many sides of a loving Father, Jesus and the Holy Spirit.

Salt can prevent a fall. God can use us to help others not to go down wrong paths. There are times when we ourselves can travel paths not helpful in our lives. But God uses everything, and we can be salt to those who are about to put their foot to a road that may be slippery.

Water baptism is also a beautiful analogy of our life dying and entering into a new life. Fully immersed in the deep waters of God's love. When we get lowered backwards it represents death to our old lives, and as we are raised up out of the water, we are raised into a new life. Our sins are washed away and our wet bodies and hair show a different life . . . we look different and we have done this in front of other people. Others have witnessed that we have made a choice to live a different way. Even obedience to be baptised.

When we are being obedient to God, this brings a joy. In our meeting one night we had a lovely sister who carries a gift of releasing joy into the group. I found that the Holy Laughter released something in me. I didn't even realise that things had attached to me and had accumulated over the years. Sometimes we are so busy 'surviving' that we fail to laugh and gain strength from our joy in Christ.

Whatever the Holy Spirit leads us to do . . . this is what will bring us joy.

Being baptised in the Spirit is not only necessary but is another tool to help us to be strong in God. As we pray in a heavenly language we experience God's Spirit communicate to ours as to what is important, what we need to pray about and what needs to take place to advance his kingdom.

May we follow in his footsteps and be obedient to his voice. May we experience his joy, joy, joy . . . deep down in our souls.

Chapter Ten
Sea Experience

1998

This part is why this book exists. This chapter is all about a vision I received from Jesus after an experience in Castlerock.

It was a beautiful summer's day and the coastline lay before us as we traversed the dunes at Castlerock, County Antrim, Northern Ireland. I had received that familiar nudge from the Trinity to set myself apart and to walk and talk with my heavenly Father, my Best Friend, Brother, Guide and Comforter.

I said to the person with me that I needed some time with God. They understood and beckoned me to walk separate from them.

As I looked out over the sea I was strangely drawn to the waves and their beauty as they crashed along the stretch of sands before me. At this point I felt that God was the sea . . . in its vastness and depth. I rolled up my jeans and started to paddle in the cool waves. The water covered my feet and soon I was up to my shins and then my knees. Each time I walked away from the water it felt like I was walking away from God's special touch.

At this point I just wanted to wade in, to be covered in his depth. It says in Psalm 42:7 that deep calls unto deep. In all my Christian years I had never felt so strongly that the depth of my spirit wished to cry out to the depths of God. Soon I was up to my waist, fully clothed, and the first fear that hit me was the fear of man. What if someone saw me and thought I was taking my life? Thankfully, I knew to ignore the fear and press on.

The next fear was that of the size of the waves as they grew higher and higher. I was reminded of the great waves of revival that God's church had encountered over the years. Each wave brought a fresh revelation of God and who he was.

The final fear was when the seaweed wrapped itself around my ankle. The Holy Spirit communicated to me that if we stand still for too long we can get caught up in the things of this world and fail to move in the things of God.

As I stood waist deep I was also reminded of the scripture in Ezekiel 47. It gives an account of being ankle deep, knee deep, waist deep and then it says that no man could endure the waters as they would pass over their head. I remembered on the way to India, God had shown me as I read that scripture that we could journey the shallow waters but the deep waters could only be tackled if we relied on Christ in us and enabling us.

I wanted to swim under the water, but I didn't and I felt sad that I couldn't do this on this occasion. I walked out of the waters and I was met by a man who was walking up the beach. He looked at me as if he had witnessed me walking into the waters fully clothed. The next thing I knew I was telling him of my encounter and speaking freely to him about God and his depths. The man said to me, 'I am a backslider and I know I need to get right with God again.' It was one of those God moments that you just couldn't write (although I guess it is being written in this book) and I thank God for that encounter with that man who had lost his way.

I walked further up the beach and soon reached a pier. I walked along it and I sat on the edge to look at hues of blue before me. I noticed marks on the side of the pier at the other side; they read 60, 70, 80 to denote the depth of water. Again, I was reminded of the depth of God and this was paralleled in the gradients of deep blue waters that lay before me.

I walked back towards the dunes to meet with my friend. They told me that when they had looked out from the dunes they had seen me and said, 'The strange thing is, when I looked out at you I had to look twice. I don't know how to say this . . . it looked as if you were walking on water!' When they said this I shared how I believed I had just had an amazing encounter with the Almighty. As I relayed this to my friend, I also relayed my sadness at not venturing further into the waters. They said, 'You will have another chance.'

The Vision

A week later I was standing in a church. I was shocked as every worship song contained some mention of water or the depth of God!

Then as we sang one worship song I closed my eyes and it was as if I was transported back to that beach. God was giving me a vision. This time I walked straight in, the waves going right over my head. In the depths of the water I saw the beautiful Trinity. I swam over to them and Father God gave me a mask to help me to breathe under water. (The representation in this is huge! Father God can help us to breathe in his depths, in his knowledge and in his revelations.)

Next, I looked and I was a mermaid. (Please don't shoot me! This is all visual and when God gives visuals he is trying to convey a message. I know that a mermaid is purely mythical.) I believe that the mermaid represented the ease to which we should swim in the deeper things of God. A mermaid does not need breathing apparatus to swim under water, and she has a tail to help her manoeuvre the deep blue seas.

In the vision I swam between the Father, Jesus and the Holy Spirit. I can't even explain the joy that this brought to my heart. Then at one point I was washed back up on the beach and I had my legs. I remember in the vision the 'No!' I released from my spirit. I wanted to be back with the Trinity. So I ran back into the water. When I got back to where the Trinity were, the Father shook his head as if to say, 'No, you can't stay here.' When I asked, 'Why?' the Father communicated with me that I must take the revelation of them back out to the world.

I found myself in the vision washed up on the beach once more with my legs firmly intact. As I looked up the beach I could see Jesus with his footprints behind him. I heard these words in my spirit:

'Follow in my footsteps.'

I received this revelation in 1998. In the following years I would place my foot in each footprint that lay before me, sometimes not even consciously. Sometimes it would be after events that I would see the parallels. I have said it before in this book – I don't feel that I am anything special. I just believe that God gave me a revelation that can be completed by anyone with a heart to follow after Jesus. In John 14:12 Jesus says, 'Very truly I tell you, whoever believes in me will do the works I have been doing, and they will do even greater things than these.' To be honest this verse scares me a little as I feel that my life is far from that of Jesus. But one thing I do know . . . I have experienced the supernatural. I have heard God speak and then perform amazing things.

All I can encourage you as a reader of this book to do is to follow after Jesus. He will not let you down or disappoint you. He will bring you an excitement that no drug on this planet can give you. He can give you a peace that no other human being can promise you, even your husband or your wife. He will remind you of why you are here, for we all have a unique destiny. He will heal your wounds and show you how to forgive the unforgiveable.

If you haven't ever followed Jesus, or had a relationship with the heavenly Father, or trusted the Holy Spirit to guide your way before now, then if you are willing you can say these words to him now.

'Heavenly Father, I want to thank you for the words that are within this book and the revelation that you love me. I accept that you sent your Son Jesus to die in my place. I recognise that I sin on a daily basis and the only thing that can take that away is the blood of Jesus Christ. Only he can wash me white as snow and wash me clean. I recognise that he is the One True High Priest and is the advocate between you and me. Thank you that because of what Jesus did on the cross I can have a relationship with you and make a difference in this world. I surrender my life to you now and ask you to use my life. Holy Spirit, I ask that you be my guide, teacher and healer. Heal anything that would hinder my walk with you. I welcome you into my heart. Walk into every room. Dine with me and make your home in me. I give you permission and I submit to your Holy Spirit. Use me, Lord, for your glory. Amen.'

If you have said these words with your whole heart then you are now a Christian, a follower of Jesus Christ. Get amongst other followers of Christ and rely on the Holy Spirit to guide your journey. Keep your spiritual ears open to God speaking to you. He can speak in many different ways.

Let others know the good news. Sorry to say that not everyone will understand how wonderful the step is that you have just taken. Some may mock you but remember that there are those who will not grasp that you have passed from one kingdom to another. If they don't rejoice, there are angels in heaven who rejoice at your decision today.

I praise Jesus in advance for the souls that have just decided to enter his kingdom. Father God is waiting with open arms.

Chapter Eleven
Revelations to Bring Hope

This chapter is all about the visions that I received from God over the years. There are visions here that brought revelation and perspective into my life, exactly when I needed it. My hope is that something in this chapter will help another to gain heavenly perspective. We all need to know that our heavenly Father is a loving God, waiting to whisper truth into our ears. Truth always sets us free and prepares us to tell others of the wonder-working power of a God who desires that we bring him our every fear and anxiety.

Be blessed as you read. May these visions minister to you.

Angry at Loss

This is one of the first visions I received when I became a Christian. I was in the heavenly throne room. I was on Father's knee and I was sitting one moment, then the next I had swung around with my fist in the air about to hit Father. I was shocked at my own action, but Father God grasped my wrist so that I didn't make contact. He said, 'You're angry with me for taking your parents.' My parents had died when I was seventeen years old, my father in the February of that year and my mother in the October. I had gone off into the world and gone away from God in an act of defiance, only to return to him, weary and exhausted from experimenting in the world for nine years.

Recognising my hidden anger helped me to let go of the pain I carried and the anger I felt towards God. Satan was only too happy for me to be angry with God. Father, of course, wanted me to be free of this anger so that our relationship could be closer and Satan couldn't have a foothold. Through this vision I was able to accept that God had his timing in taking our loved ones. Both my parents were Christians, so I didn't have that pain in my heart; it was more an anger that I didn't get to have them at a wedding or the important stages of my life. That day I let go. I came to understand that, in a way, God had formed me to walk forward, to be strong and to be fathered and mothered by HIM. He guided me to pray against an 'orphan spirit' and later I would see the significance of being quite an independent soul, which at times is good. But God never intends us to be so independent that we are not team minded, so he healed me of an independent spirit also. I now relish in 'Team' as I love bringing out others' gifts. Also, as we work together we do not need to feel so alone. God has surrounded me with beautiful brothers and sisters in Christ.

Covenant Relationship

Again, I was on Father God's knee. Father's hand moved across the front of my eyes. I noticed a ring on his finger. I asked, 'What is that?' He said, 'That is my ring, I am married to you.' God was communicating his covenant relationship with me/us/nations.

In Haggai 2;23 it says, '"On that day," declares the LORD Almighty, "I will take you, my servant Zerubbabel, son of Shealtiel," declares the LORD, and I will make you like my signet ring, for I have chosen you," declares the LORD Almighty.'

The signet ring was the king's ring. His seal was engraved on it and it held power to set seals and send forth edicts. It represented the king's authority.

When Abraham's servant gave Rebekah a nose ring, it was to claim her as a bride.

Both ring types are God's communication to us. We are his bride; he is covenanted to us as he is to Israel. He also is our King who holds great power. In years gone by kings sealed documents with their rings and wax. We have a God who seals everything he communicates to us.

An edict is an official order or proclamation issued by a person in authority. Father God proclaims ownership over us, but not in a slavery type fashion. No, more like a loving act of 'I am his and he is mine', more like a Solomon's cry of the heart. HE is the lover of our souls.

Weebles Wobble But They Don't Fall Down

This vision is about the Holy Spirit. I was passing through some healing regarding loneliness. God had brought me back to a moment in my childhood where I was on my own. In the memory I sat with my Weebles on the floor (little egg-shaped characters with little faces; the advertisement for them chimed out 'Weebles wobble but they don't fall down'). I was busying myself creating little stories as I took my egg-shaped friends to the circus or sent them out in their little caravan on a holiday.

I looked and saw a figure on the bed. I said to Father, 'Who is that?' He said, 'That is the Holy Spirit. When I said that I would never leave you or forsake you – I meant it.' I can honestly say that any sense of loneliness left me on that day. I have watched myself go to places on my own that others would say, 'Are you ok on your own?' How wonderful is the love and guidance of our beautiful Holy Spirit. He is there – always – so that we don't have to wobble in life.

Dance for Joy

Again, this vision is about the Holy Spirit. I was in a small gathering in a house meeting and things had gone a bit 'religious'. I looked and saw the Holy Spirit at the top part of the living room. He was 'getting on down' in dance. I actually laughed out loud and got some disapproving glances from people around me. I can't stress this enough . . . the Holy Spirit knew how to enjoy himself. He exuded joy and also all seriousness had gone out the window. Sometimes, people, we just need a good laugh and a good dance. We can become too religious. Let's loosen up church. Jesus is coming back for a spotless bride, but one that knows how to dance. Amen.

Eyes of Fire

I was in a congregation with brothers and sisters in Christ. In the midst of the worship I saw Jesus on a great white horse. There was blood on the bottom part of his robes. I looked and from his eyes came lasers of fire. It felt like the great time of judgement was happening. I was so struck by the fact that thousands of years ago Jesus had come as a lamb in order to gain our salvation. Now he was a mighty warrior, coming to judge and bring freedom for his bride. Hallelujah!

Streets of Gold

In this vision I was in a chariot. The horses were mighty; I could see and hear their strength. I looked and they had brought me to the gates of heaven. I stepped out and entered in through the gates and, once inside heaven, I saw the streets of gold. Father God said, 'There is coming a time when these streets are no longer needed as I will form a new heaven and a new earth. Call down the gold from heaven for my kingdom purposes.' As Father God spoke I heard the horses outside making that noise that horses make from their nostrils. There was such a sense of power from these horses. I even felt that they were end-time horses and, of course, I was reminded of Elijah as he was taken up to glory in a chariot.

I believe we have the authority to call down provision from heaven. In order to advance God's kingdom we need money. It was clear that we just had to believe . . . and call it down.

Chapter Twelve
The Final Chapter

I believe we are in the final chapter of the age, namely the book of Revelation. Whatever you may believe regarding the scriptures – and there are many different interpretations of Revelation – the signs of the times are here. Recently, the whole world practically ground to a halt for a pandemic, and in relation to nation rising against nation, as it says in Matthew 24:6-8, 'You will hear of wars and rumours of wars, but see to it that you are not alarmed. Such things must happen, but the end is still to come. Nation will rise against nation, and kingdom against kingdom. There will be famines and earthquakes in various places. All these are the beginning of birth pains.'

It is in these days that as Christians we can pray the darkness back as we are not yet in the tribulation, but we are witnessing a lead up to it with all we see around us.

It is interesting that Jesus says, 'Do not be alarmed.' So, when news is put out from the media, we must be wise as to what we believe and we are not to be alarmed because, it is written, these things will happen before Jesus returns. So as his bride, instead of concerning ourselves with whatever the news would scare us with, being mindful to pray for those trapped in threatening situations, we just need to get ourselves ready for the bridegroom.

Recently, God showed me that he is asking us to de-clutter and enter through a small door. In July 2021 I stood at a picture of a house that had been draped at a seaside resort to depict a time when the houses would be built and stand there instead of the banner. I had jokingly bent over, reached for the handle, and the shot was taken. In the photo you can see me trying to enter a small door of a house.

One month later, my husband and I separated, but reconciled three months later. In this process we downsized from a three-bedroom to a two-bedroom house.

Months previously I had prayed, asking God to open doors for us to live somewhere that we could grow vegetables and even prepare for more difficult days ahead. I knew at some point we would walk through a time where we could not buy or sell. Indeed, God will sustain his children, even supernaturally. Are we to recognise that God gave manna from heaven to the Israelites and not believe that he will supernaturally provide for us also? Will he not also stretch our food, like the fish and the loaves, when the time comes?

I believe he will, but I also felt in my spirit that in these last days, he wishes to position his people and we must be willing to go wherever he sends us, because there will be a tribe of people who we will need to connect with, and those connections will be very special and very powerful.

Let me be clear, God did not cause our separation, but rather he wove it into the tapestry of our complicated lives and helped us to downsize.

In our case, God shifted us to Ballyhalbert. This is a seaside village and the people are the friendliest I've ever meet. There is a wonderful sense of community and people go out of their way to help you.

In the midst of moving locations God helped us to face head on the issues we had. Marriage is meant to be one of the most beautiful unions, but in our case various issues had threatened to break that union (which I'm not divulging in this book, but God knows and God sees). The two lovebirds that God himself had called together and gave a wedding date of 29th June 2020 (which, by the way, was in the middle of Covid). We had twenty-eight people in our garden on the day that the government allowed thirty people at an outdoor event. In the midst of a storm in the morning, by the time we stood at the city hall the sun shone. You see different factors may try to break a union, but if God has put together two people, then God help anyone or anything that tries to come against that union. That also included us.

When we reconciled, we worked through our issues one by one. It had also led me to take out a year lease on a place in Belfast just before our marriage had reconciled. Thankfully this did not go to waste and God used the Garden Apartment for a house group. It was called 'The Retreat House Group'. We then had a group in Ballyhalbert, smaller in number, but good powerful connections. At both meetings we met, praised and prayed to the Father, Son and Holy Spirit. God had given me a remit. The groups were for 'the hungry, the thirsty and those feeling isolated'.

So out of all the brokenness God had brought many resolutions. God was using the broken vessels. I think this is very encouraging for any reader. You don't have to be completely fixed before he uses you, but God takes his broken vessels and makes a message out of our mess.

We can see that it is not about being perfect (although we are encouraged to be perfect as he is perfect), but rather others can take heart that in our weakness we are made strong (see 2 Corinthians 12:10).

So back to the de-cluttering. Often, we possess many things that we do not need. God kept showing me a large needle that sat on a unit beside me, and I was reminded of the scripture in Matthew 19:24, 'Again I tell you, it is easier for a camel to go through the eye of a needle than for someone who is rich to enter the kingdom of God.' In biblical times camels were heavily loaded with goods and riders. They would need to be unloaded in order to pass through any city gate. Therefore, the analogy is that a rich man would have to similarly unload his material possessions in order to enter heaven.

When we had to leave the three-bedroom house, we were overwhelmed as to what we had accumulated. None of us needs half the things that we own. We are still de-cluttering!

It also needs to be said that being rich does not keep you out of heaven, as when we read further in this passage it says, 'With God all things are possible' (v.26), but rather this is about heart attitudes and what we do with our wealth. Will we share it? Also having 'things' will never bring us lasting peace, only Jesus will. This may sound like a cliché, but it is true. Only his presence will bring us a peace that passes anything this world can offer.

It doesn't surprise me that in this final chapter about following Jesus it is about de-cluttering and putting our money where our mouth is. In these last days God is asking us to throw off everything that would stand in our way.

I will end with Hebrews 12:1, 'Therefore, since we are surrounded by such a great cloud of witnesses, let us throw off everything that hinders and the sin that so easily entangles. And let us run with perseverance the race marked out for us.'

We each have a race *marked out for us*. May we discern it and run our races with a holy confidence.